LinguaQuake

rubbery like incalculable glue

rubbery like incalculable

carillon careen
cactus purpling

a relic of perfidies
a perfidious relic

L

IN

GUA

Q U

A K E

Heller Levinson

Joseph S. Phillips and Susan J. Wood, Ph.D., Publishers
www.blackwidowpress.com

Cover Artwork: Quarry, VIII (detail) by Linda Lynch, Pastel pigment on cotton paper, 60 x 44 inches, 2015
Cover design: Linda Lynch
Artwork, page 41: Karst Drawing by Linda Lynch, Pastel pigment on cotton paper in nine panels, 90 x 132 inches, 2017

Book production: Kerrie L. Kemperman

ISBN-13: 978-0-9995803-3-2

Printed in the United States
10 9 8 7 6 5 4 3 2 1

for Will Alexander

the Query *situates* the Evaporate

Table of Condemnations

* We will obliterate the traditional "table of contents" & replace it with the "table of condemnations," claiming that: The traditional "table of contents" is a leftover hierarchical, divisive tool hiving the mind into suffocative categories straight-jacketed by subject matter. Opposed to cloistering the 'subject' into comfortable cocoons, convenient Sanitization Stations, the *Quake* will have breaks, highs & lows, pauses, gaps, elisions, lacunae… more resembling Breath than catalogue.

* The Image is Dead:
The notion that poetry is "largely about the juxtaposition of images" (i.e., 'the neon jukebox') is antiquated. What qualifies as 'poetry' for one period of time does not insure its validity for all time. The image has been treated brilliantly by outstanding poets such as Aimé Césaire, André Breton, Hart Crane, Emily Dickinson, Isidore-Lucien Ducasse, among countless others. The Image has reigned supremely & now must expire gracefully. To employ imagistic strategy at this point in time is to be overly reliant on other's loadstones. It is to be dependent, unoriginal, & stale. Most importantly, it is to impair the urge to discover new approaches for Fresh Revelations. It is to compromise the art with reflex conditioning rather than exploratory enterprise.

The formerly fertile is now the wilted & unimaginative.

* Instead of 'footnotes' or 'endnotes' which specify a locality, we will opt for the term 'Spray' which is concurrent & en-circling, a misty omni-whereness.

* We will now abandon "listing" condemnations & permit them to blister forth unrestricted in the following pages.

LinguaQuake(s) Emerging

* Modular Collapse: we will see modules morph, liquidate, & interosculate in multiple capacities. They will self-destruct. They will convulse. They will mangle & entangle. "Splinter (p. 38)," a reformulation imposer, exemplifies MC (see Spray, 7a).

* Chaotic Symmetry: the apparently slip-shod & disorderly is integral to the Entirety of an Organism's Lively Burgeon.

Autopoietic systems theory understands that "Gaia can flip out, in system collapse after system collapse; there are limits to the power of systemic processes of homeostasis and reformulating order out of chaos at ever more complex levels. Complexity can unravel; earth can die. It matters to become response-able." (see Donna J. Haraway's *Staying with the Trouble: Making Kin in the Chthulucene*)

* The applications swirl to & away from, whirl in Looping SuperconDuctive CorrelaTives. To designate each poem to its own page is to deliver an estranged carcass. That is Literary Segregation. Prejudice aimed at the poetic groin.

tenebrous stone wrack

     churl

     lip-lull

     russet wagon   rune-rustle warble   remunerate

rodomontade

harnessed to chlorophyll axioms

to an Alexandrian demeanor

the breath abates

in the manner of

marches, ;   this too

                   , dusty lairs

                   , undergarments

                    , slick pebble impound

jeweled alligator breath constitutes

flame retardancy

where in the

dispatch

is

solemnity

vigor: a game changer

keypads clearly

                              ,   the sum of things

    : of all the arts today, *truancy* is the most overlooked. being

other   than the supposed. the talent to arrive. *there.*

otherly = motherly

contemplate "arrivals" under the mantle of:

"delayed"

"on time"

how much of

time

is

'characterized'

the scrutinized ://: the inscrutable

collective foils

anneal annex approbate appendix

appropri – ately

shook slumber alimentary stalk

. it all adds up

. in a manner of

beseech betwixt besmirch

consider distance[i]

consider disruption

consider the attraction of opposites

consider: agriculture's role in global warming[ii]

ataraxia bumble bee boondoggle boomerang

— bumptious cloth

lost & found: excavate

                         bring forth

extrude

ex-hume

hum-an-i-ty

jurisprudence   the constitution of roller skates

— roll rock rigmarole glissade galaxy

— ragamuffin

baleful buffoon

cha cha dawns peremptorize heel splash squall squadron the
mighty

burnish emerald

falsifications fail to testify

this too, Mr. Phillips, preemption is a strike against underbelly a

lack of consideration for the seemly matriculation is the way to

go

liturgy traipses the designated the designated are undecided

peculiarity has its own massage

— the motherland hosts the pathos games

burl lash omnidriver precipitous palpitate

    lark

     leer

     luminosity

no longer fit for comedic theater

no longer fit

subsidize

with assembly out of which,

pertinence, as it pertains,

pertinacity plugs a moot pugilism

pugnacious   peremptory   preliminary

the road to horror road   horrified stitch

        horrification scarified

ditch udderadderrudderspoke utter

ly   adumbrative

it all adds up

the sum of things

bear witness

 as such

tenebraed to

distance

& if but this was here

steps   accumulate

        :: canister bee ::

[if one is where one is is distance a fiction ; a tale ; a flirtation

[no gaps just changed positions

[body as spatial block   as stampeding curtail   But

what got us here

deep in the path of scarlet horseshoe

reversibility & the day of the Cyprians

place: a consideration

or

a position

to map

: :

where in the

map

is the

query

the wobble   the displaced the

misplaced the wayward the

awkward the maligned the

malignant the belligerent the allergenic the tame the footloose

the fancy free the frolicsome the remote smote freeload reload

download

upload explode

the road to lost road

epoxy garlic   restraints uneasy

no longer fabric   catalytic sustenant

billow   canopy-cut

passing lanes squirt mongoose

churlish with zoology the engine spits

meters equipment

                              rough trade

                    counterfeit curves

vehicular inspections on a regular basis

identity races

the chord finds its way

tenebraed to

slant

perspicuous proclivity

plunge   prune parabola

pawn giraffe

rice-needle the cackle of encumber

afoot

something afoot

if only but where the do does

      where-withal

      derive

      derivation

slant cock-eyed astern fathom

unperturbed seemingly without frustration frustration-free

unencumbered fustian cloth the geometry of horizons daily fruit

baskets aplenty

forthcoming

coming forth   to the foreground   slant forward slant rear toward carti-

lage depravity

superior privileges start with the over-privileged

rubber foxes hose the way

My Memoir:

I am writing my memoir. My occlusion is complete. My devas-

tation forthcoming. Memoir processes the memorable. Glued

to the ineffable, I bluster for breath. For orientation. For a way

to handover hand down my memoir. My memoir is becoming

very precious to me. For only I can write it. My memoir is someone else's biography. Someone else's biography can grow on the back of my memoir. Obedience as a way of life. I strive to be obedient to my memoir. To pay it full attention. To honor its focus which is, myself. The myself that shutters itself in brimstone. that cackles during fornication. that deposits fecal matter in hallowed halls. that slithers around astral bodies remunerates the dead & repairs appendages of underwater panthers. this I which is an incinerate pustulant is up for grabs. I mean to grab it. to tame it. temper it. equip it for the pages of my memoir. I want my memoir to be sterling & memorable. to be a manifesto of Me-ness. of the best of me. even the worst of me if it serves to sparkle the pages. for enticing is everything. it must bedazzle. dazzling sells. it is important to sell. to reap huge sales. for that establishes the me I am addressing. to deliver a me that does not sell is to place the I in predicament. an I that fails to proceed. that fails to attract. that shrink-wraps into obscurity. the me that I am dedicated to memorialize is failing to appear. this is a monumental problem. the biograph(ies)y may precede my memoir. which guarantees to distort the me I am devoted to. how can a biography be true to the facts if the facts have yet to appear. facts fail to appear because the me is absent. the biography of absence. perhaps the memoir I am dedicated to bring forth would have more success as an adventure story. the remarkable search for the missing me.

tenebraed to

nitrogen[iii]

the cyclically alimentative

dis-charge

in-charge

soluble

"Ironically, that the same substance – nitrates – was essential to improving agricultural yields *and* to making explosives."

how much of cyclicality

is

rasp…

rub frisson splay, that between the spots fertilizer, fricative-

tantalize

essentially the dialogue as framework : call & response : the

inter-

gather : in-gest ://: di-gest : the insupportable supported,

the supported → suspect

the road to nutritive road

shanghaied

buried deep within the flagellative, from the

undergird of a failed prehistory

      fetid squall

      foiled surrogate

the cast-offs no longer supplemental

insufficiency the new mandate

tankers off the coast slog on

to have a self that fails to materialize when your livelihood

depends on the sales of your memoir is hardly a laughing matter.

memoir privileges the me. Am I condemned to an under-

privileged me? servicing the underprivileged. I must stop

feeling sorry for myself. It impedes forward motion. Induces

paralysis. caretakes impotency. no. the endeavor requires

massaging the me into a respectable I. an I of stature.

captivating. over-towering. an I an I can proudly *go forth* with.

beaded through   cerulean

breaths

        a pause

grappling with tongue-tied

shorelines

look

casts off   interlocks   simmers

ward of the look

tenderize

dismantle

comingle

enter

prise

~~~~~~~~~~~~~~~   333   e _____ ***************

m   564 456 645   b +++++++++++++++

o   232323232/3   l

        den

enterprise + embolden = initiative

enterprise minus initiative = stale

initiative minus embolden = mediocre

standardization

byline

triumphalism

an out-of-date line-up trumps the legs of mercy as if only so

much as if to qualify the critters flail over yonder by the by

under turnstile through perpendicular the rectory the intelligible

usages of oxygen on a dare you speak otherwise as a matter of

fact only the lonely the brave require gasoline seal the bolts chin

up flabby folk fold easy there for the taking backward flying

birds sanctuarize homesteads cede to succeed the succulence

emerging indemnity the cost of clouds qualifications

overlooked pass the cheese duodenum doodle dolorous please if

only if only so much butter in dependable count on it you are

what you what you are no briefly really only here for the monu-

mental momentary flings fly casual bibelot bumptious bravado bluster bratwurst burp

   bombastic even   gently the doors have floors have knobs

roofs movable things no similes can account for the price of salt

the question

remains is it

seaworthy

shadows

casting for breeze

crave

to

flu-tter

flutter

ag   i   ta   tion

          dis-turb   twitch

un   du   late

flutteration pins me. I am comatose. broke. a slag upon the

floor. low down. my delusions my dreams smattered. to be. to

be all you can be. haunts me. I crave to measure up. to amount

to something. to become. to to to   yes, to formulate. to emerge.

hell, if not to *be,* — to resemble?

above board   clearance   clearing   transparent

   all aboard   above all surmount   call all   open book

testimony swearing-in   underoveryonderclover   dovestipple

                         tripleply

underhandedundertow   how low can you go

underdog   underworld

sub-terranean

      subterfuge

      sub-average

      sassafrass

unerring sl(e)ights to the whiff-pistil

calculations floppy no longer sus

tain remote the handhelds the cookie-crumbs lapsing frayed

allegiances

forfeit

the ebb-hearted

leave

town

surety

to be sure   surely righto

          Truth or Consequences

surely the odds are   the benefits outweigh

does sure breed adamant?

surety struts before frangible

on the shores of surety truism floats

unlikely plots the postman turbulence a virtue way of life

mustard seed clearly prismspolyhedronsasparagushouseofcards

unruliness got us here way to go horse feather bridle the path

look downside at right angles sensible makes sense only if

the wager if only moreover hardly sometimes of if ever obviously

otherwise combustible don't fret the stain can be removed

splinter

off   tear off   come away from   undone (so many forms/formula-

tions to undone: peel away; shave-off,…)

"a needlelike piece split or rent off lengthwise" (*Webster's Third*)

a break a split   an em-bark-ation

    where in the

    splinter

is

surge

speak[iv]

utterance   skiff-breeze-whiffle

speak to

] is speech a verbal handshake, a reach-out

    a cover-up, a life-surge-dampener, a shallow rind

    obscuring the unspoken gristle-covenant.

     a settling, a putting to order, a form of stow-away

] speaking to oneself is yet a speaking to

] is mumbling speech inhibited

"The Expressed Expresses The Inability To State What Is Said

In The Unsaid."[v]

abyss smoulder

tenebrous masks

slickened parentheses

if only but then this too clear as butter flutter ring

agitate numberless queer eggs postulate once curly grind

foregrounds come up short only the lonely recitative definitively

fill in the blanks at home score so much game behind the rind

couldn't be other than other along the way pebbling & such

Dear Heller,

This last week was the first week of truly returning to drawing. I'd been conjuring for days, weeks, prior to returning to the studio, where I wanted to begin again. It was to return to the *Quarry Drawings* and to do one on a monumental scale.

I tacked up the nine panels that fill the entire end wall of my studio, 7.5 x 11 feet of paper. As I began laying out the feeling of the drawing in light pencil I was pondering where I'd left *quarry* so many months back. But another word – another *concept* – began to insistently arise from very deep, pushing and pushing its way up to my consciousness. The word was *karst*. When it reached my mind clearly and finally I thought to myself that I didn't really know, or couldn't remember, what *karst* was. What was it? It was so insistent. It pushed *quarry* right out of my head and landed in my studio with a pronounced arrival. I grabbed my phone and tapped in: "Define: karst" and was taken aback to read:

"Karst is a special type of landscape that is formed by the dissolution of soluble rocks, including limestone and dolomite. Karst regions contain aquifers that are capable of providing large supplies of water. … Natural features of the landscape such as caves and springs are typical of karst regions. Karst landscapes are often spectacularly scenic areas. Examples include the sinkhole plains and caves of Kentucky, the large crystal-clear springs of Florida, and the complex, beautifully decorated caves of New Mexico." (*Karst Waters Institute*).

A literal chill ran across me. Karst was about everything I had recently been through and everything ancient in my personal history. It encompasses not only the *Quarry Drawings,* but *Bone Springs Rain Grass* and *Goat Seep,* and essentially the entire history of my drawing practice. It is something I feel I understand on a deep primordial level and it welled up and revealed itself.

LL

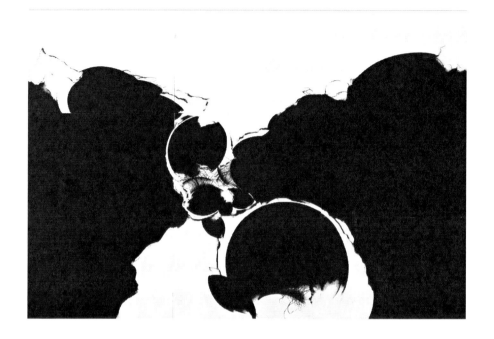

from stone this running

→ Karst

strickening aperture bleed-storm   monumental ambidexterity

lighting

lightening

strike-a-light

crushed quizzicals bleed to purge to cross cross-over verge

converge

emerge   b l e n d

turn return crush compound   everywhere a god if only

from storm this stone   caulk cauldron caul   encoilclusterclub

enmesh   molar-webs-Terpsichore   fraught figurations

concoctions

concocting

where in the

interloper

is

property management

the overly deliberative forfeit foot-smash-

fallacy-hammer

Jack Daniels

loosed in the trammel path of aubergine witness bearers pause

for

serendipity a polished splash delights misfits   monks   mustangs

stretched across sear the

dollop-bruise revelator

it's a terrible admission. a clear statement of defeat. that in the

face of my rank inability to create a serviceable me, I would settle

for a resemblance. not a true me but some facsimile of a me. a

surrogate. a stand-in. a ghost.

to resemble is to appear like. not to be *that* but to *appear* to be

that. you are not *being* but appearing. one's being is flunking

being.

Sympoiesis: "making with." I think I have been misled. Nothing

comes from nothing. I have been seeking to "make" in isolation.

acting in accordance with self-organizing principles. clearly

inadequate to the task. to request a self that is not a self to

create a self. absurd. now a light at the end of the tunnel. a

beckoning. I can do it. I think I can do it. all I need is a partner.

a knead-together.

splinter[vi]

       → rip

ped from lodgment

lone isolate

       giddy in

the un-hook

     splinter ~ f l u t t e r s through

the

dismantle

parting[vii]   pulled from   wrench oblong

peel   shave-off   look back (a nod, a longing, regret, release)

splinter imparts to the departed a leave-behind, → in its act of

splintering, splinters the splintered-from → a two-part

Identity Reconstruction:

] the Splinter in its disengagement flares into the Open[viii]

where in the going, the release, is the guidance

] the Splintered-From, stripped, degraded by loss, — Or —

enhanced by un-burden, a salubrious *shedding* (shudderformulative, , ,

:: both now grounded in *shap-ing*

how to 'speak', then, for the thing splintered (see Spray, 7c), to

honor the *inci-dents,* the bio-dynamics of *shaping,* to forage there,

in Ac

Tiv I Ty

stab at splinter-hood: flesh-pierce, *Homo sapiens* commingle, flesh-

embed, blood-wetted, ported by ambulation,

(remarking upon dis-placement) … poked, scratched-at, →

pried[ix]

relying heavily on graph analysis I plot my mate. I am exalted.

fluttering with anticipation. possibility. I am on my way to be-

coming someone. soon to emerge. into. *person-hood*. I cannot

stress this too strongly. how thrilling it is. to be *about to*. on the

cusp. of. hatching. pages pages pages. I am visualizing pages

filled with my *Self*. who wouldn't be giddy. after years of depri-

vation. submerged. an obliterate in a sea of commotion.

portability

weighted this way that way   crepuscularalbinofloss

flirtations signal sluice magnetic hoofbeats   pow-wow in

vermillion   carried away   curl curvature tiger crouch blue

skies of Kentucky take a train run amok trunk atoll truck island

hop crowbar craze dash along ambulate

sated

tasty circumference chew

so obvious. right before me. grist. gristle. frisson. → gal vin i

za tion. all that was needed. required. the Other. to rub

against. to agitate into being. there's the rub. from the roots of

ancient fire practice. to begin. to start. ignite. rub one against

the other. rub-a-dub-dub,... .

the trail to famished trail[x]

esurient devise   oneiric[xi] spool

windings wound palaver flesh,

                                        harbinger swarm

cuttle-walk   cod-wattle

the road to incident road

— trilling trail-wise —

follow the ravens

at the intersection of runic flare-up a

smaragdine sustain

. the stuff of buttons

. lace-work

. loop rodeo

salivary vector planes helix whorl wreathe weave

the road to incident road   cataract

conjunct   conjoin   co-ordinates

acquisition. acquiring the *mate*. the constitution that can con-

struct a verifiable me. the thrill of the hunt. the trail. to embark

upon this adventure into self-hood. bringing to bear that which

will manifest will actually actualize a substantive ME. there. I

have identified a solution.

herding silence

through

thistle   bramble   brine

city clatter

heel-nips

to

tuck back

into

place

      [place as a candidacy, as a bunching, as the stake-out

      that qualifies

footbeats

pounding

vacuum

lustre

baronial   burnish

         baronial burnish discharge   belly-wag

                             log-lolly

   : to possess lustre : : to be possessed *by* lustre : illuminated

with : one-eyed dormancies

to bring to a _____

the state/condition of _____

to festoon in the membrane of sheen, accessorize, exalt beyond

the boundary of skin

fin-glimmer fantail frigate furl

purling underwater opal gardens

fantasias inflame

the ash

slip

= pronounced slide

alacritous disarray

        peel-forth sputter in sin u ate   *glide*

coax assemble no pattern but

blend

Calder mobiles detach

breeze away

glide like itinerant mist

serried-pop sussurus slur

           ausculate

spill

    sleigh

                                slip

                          slide

    s   e   e   p   slur   swirl swish

purl broth bauble bob

                    bor-e-a-lis

burble broil   breast-stroke   bombinate

glissade tremolo glottis glide

                                tuck & roll

                                bob & weave

larval throb

lurch griddle

suds sizzle

stride slipper wave-lap plasmic guttural twirl curl

twizzle swizzle spiral serpentine coil morph

                                          horizontal bars

                                          3-In-One oil

                                          hydroblade

molt

molten

meander

melt

glide   glee   full

ly   larch lurch lupus lair

lungy lozenge whorl

loose susurrus strut sward

                    sluice slice

sloop John B

                    . . .

                    round reggae reign

raga

                    r a p s c a l l i o n

sermon shun   shindig souse

silly rouse ramarama rambunctious rout

, slide guitar , Son House →   lickety-split dirk doodle dad

whiskey flounce

feather flush

fra-tern-ize

fly-away

feckless

the causeway pocked with the scurvy of absentee landjuice the

landlords dusty with anemic orthodoxies witness the geometries

of collapse witness the Bedouin ark with its hull of compressed

barbiturates the hallowed Krishna with irreversible knee-rot the

cushioned elite concaving before the dread of ubiquitous equal-

ity the dredged-up drowned-down sullen woebegone skulldug-

geries consanguineous heresies trophic serum purloin before

dawn a pimpled populism plasters prickly fetches a rash of

fetishisms foiled annunciations you are early you are late you are

just on time

unnamable

loosely emanative

Emily Dickinson: "To tell the Beauty would decrease/to state the Spell demean …"

there you have it →

arch preservative   distillate wane

                    lights out

perambulate sluice juice

Beckett: "It will be the silence, where I am? I don't know: in the silence you don't know."

silence: noise squeezed shut

where in the

lustre

is

constituency

surmises slip the turnstiles

       eel clot

absenting the road to nullity road

flotation

flotation

silence

shuttered   clap collapse   leaves lifting in

tutu relevé

echoes lisp along the wall come without grudge

rock slaps rock

the disputation unaware of the voluminosity of air

deep within the crevice the heartbeat of vanish   hardly a

moment goes by that disappearance appears without rain

perpetual-reverie-lap capped

by perpendiculars bearing no purpose the

seas oblige

Red Horses appear at my doorstep. they are told no one is at

home. they disappear over the ridge. they confront me in their

dreams. but only rarely.

but only rarely newly configured without warrant demise desire

distrust the rails rusty no longer this a fiction a slice of partisan-

ship but choo choo moments of silence for the Chinese river

dolphin, the baiji,[xii] electroshocked the sprint to industrialize

compromise overturned by committee the currency demagogues

overlord iron fist fraught with tremble tremor terror totalitarian

rout mandibular ferocity chews the day wins the dame puncture

deflates the dieticians dish-out cyanide swallowing *beliefs* =

poison

arousal & the nature of

abundance

where

do   we   go

from

here

stumble

a wobble a

come upon

speech stumble = mumble

in the pitch of an irreverent aberrance this way that way grab the

booty reckon the fall ruckus the muck factor WORds

lost, adrift, vertiginous,   *way-ward*

in the grip of a higher analysis

come to grips

where in the

wayward

is the

toward

: meaning is demeaning because

   it never means much   :

in the pitch of an irreverent aberrance

abeyance   recourse

                              the

assessments poised for re-consideration

                                        gruntled slop-

sustain

        ... swerves of preservative in the dark ungulate of dank

demeanor

midst aqueducts of failed pieties flex the asphalt syndrome

promote tertiary glands to a higher order

abbreviations flatter

the plotters

blue   yonder field scope cornstalk blue moon horse Kentucky

blues Cezanne smock blue[xiii] loam rivulet roar run larval lagoon

upsweep cantilever blue Dalmatian drops blueberry woods

during the bluest of summers bluebells cornucopia blue

moussed with white colour-whipping skyscape calendric

cumulous lees the blue sharks prosper the seas indigo dyed

séance uniforms for the weary blue dolphin shoes suede

rhapsody blossom blue bosom blue pubic blue purl blue rafters

gulp blue bucketful glee to the blue-necked giraffes locked in

merry pavane merriment in the hills merriment on the seas the

stuff denim guitar field blues moan

for

in the broth of a lower order determinacy

fits/starts/fissures/flops

grip-scrambling frenetecisms court the cordiality of restored

slatterns, slum-scribes tally → subscriptions are up

ratchet swab dearth squabble, — interiority pronounced

invalid… belching a vehement anti-claim

technicolored snowstorms animate red fox recreational realias

advanced abracadabras azure-grazed thrush-warbling dithyra-

mbs rouse delerial drench reel-tumble dissonant delicacies to

swab redundancy congregations spurious while sacrosanct rev

percussives peel-blister through wind-wizard parade stomp

in the brooch-brood of quantum cross-correlatives

congeal anneal rapprochement   boot root baronial buoyancy

          word-bits qubit queing   → the grope that addles

bit stacking:

seepage/slip/step/drift/roam/wander/loaf/vacuity/imponder-

able/tangle/morass/bundlebunglebromidehuddle

seeing eye to eye with the black-spotted pufferfish

salutations to the

merge mesh meritorious multiplicitous phlogiston rhumba

her love for him was intense, everlasting. but as way leads on to

way, he being the way he be, her offering was squandered, barely

considered. her love, though, being the love love loves, glowed,

& glowed,… & glowed.

in the dank of a dark determinacy

becloud obdurate mayhem muck   Les Misérables

"This is my favorite type of night,… bien noir."

"client-based" resumes the charade of oxidization parting waters

permits prepositional sinking of the 'of the' outing of the with –

with-out – linguistic compacting encages the nomad a plea to

the ruminant to maintain color there is no holiness without holy

water truisms exist despite curvilinear basis points point to the

way getting there could be a hoot if you've got the heart pronged

to an earlier deliberation these cases in point so little of this con-

tributes but then the stuff of dreams

is largely

tenebraed to manqué. I am beside myself. my bubble burst just

like that, — presto. I was all set. on the verge. *just about* to

bloom into a *Some-Body.* ah, how rapturous it sounded. how

delightful the reverie. only to discover. in the midst of self-

actualizing bliss. that I am stalled. I am stalled in my search for

a mate that would suit me because I cannot evaluate what type

of person would suit a person who is Not. how can a Not pro-

file themselves. how can you *appeal.*   you cannot track a trail if

you don't know what you are tracking. I am the huntsman of

emptiness.

Hinge By The Slice

The suggestion that I write a short summary of Hinge Theory threw me into a tailspin. The thought of shortening an ever-expanding & en-fleshing behaviorism was anathema. Then the idea occurred that perhaps by indicating how HT resists shrivellization/ contraction/ summarization, I could approach summarization.

Language is aLive. This is foundational to HT. It should be asked: not what HT *Is*, but how it *beHaves*. Language as a living organism is continuously interactive with other organisms breeding extensively & engendering complementarity. Dr. Mary Newell puts it this way: "The connectivities of Hinge Theory introduce an intentional and generative biasing, like a pool table with all the balls commotioning and someone lifting the pool table slightly so all that activity is directed yet responsive to unpredicted collisions, meanderings, & swerve. (With the additional image that new balls are being added all the time as the pool table itself enlarges)."

Hinge does not purport to bring anything new to the proverbial 'table.' Rather it seeks to restore Language's Original Primal

Fire. To ignite the word, Hinge employs the module which is a word or a configuration of words that serves to spring (to un-leash, to unmoor) the subject into a climate of free fall & unpre-dictability. & by free fall we mean that we are liberating the subject[1]/word from its normative, conventional context & toss-ing it into question, tumbling it deconditioned into the void. A few of the modules in use are: *with, smelling, the road to _____ road, in the ____ of _____, fecundating rotational clusters, fusion reconnoiters,* & the most recent, *tenebraed,* catalyzes an entire book. When word inosculates/alchemizes word,[2] the compo-nents never lock into place nor do they dissolve into a random turbulence; they both formulate & unravel simultaneously, em-blazoned with the Living-Hood of continuous Motility. The frisson (the rub) of word against word scatters the 'particle' multi-directionally.[3] Partnering with the 'scatter' is the 'gather,' a recombinatory process regrouping the components in corre-spondence with vibrational adhesion (a form of viscous bonding).

---

[1] HT terms the subject being investigated the 'particle.'
[2] At the level of Hinge Production, each word insists on its word associates. In this sense, the practice of the author is to detect (to identify) the reproductive impulses inherent in the word being witnessed.
[3] For example, in the most recent volume, *tenebraed,* the module 'tenebraed to lamentation' undergoes three mutations or treatments.

Each particle/subject gathers into cohesions, a grouping, what Hinge terms the 'application,' formerly the 'poem.' This gathering should be seen as an alighting, a momentary pause, tensiled to soar again at the slightest provocation.[4]

The word, by undergoing a multitude of these Modular Chamberings, is in an ongoing state of emboldening/ densification/ complementarity/ & extensionality. For example, "Mermaid" has undergone over 45 applications, swiveling in the alterior ethers of: "with mermaid," "the road to mermaid road," "smelling mermaid," "in the purse of mermaid," "tenebraed to mermaid," to cite just a few. Each application both creates its own Mermaid Personality (ether) & interacts/impacts with the other applications. The Particle is always in transition, always on the road to developmental road, shimmering to fulfillment in compounding complementary refractions. Hinge Theory clashes against the current cult of quick-click-reduce, or, of what I like to term the lexiconically static. The Lexicon is a logos abuser, the enemy of the vigorous & dynamic; it is, indeed, a Dynamic Inhibitor.

---

4 The provocation here would refer to Modular Ignition.

Case in point: in *Webster's Third*, "Melancholia" & its variations take up about 4 inches of definition whereas *Melancholia: Hinge as Innominate Limina*[5] employs 99 pages to *begin* the investigation (& I term this endeavor to "investigate" an urge to "mobilize" the logos rather than "staticize" it). & these 99 pages should be viewed as just that — a prelude, an introduction, a wind-up to ignite. There is no such thing as a finish to these explorations, no endings, … they are not sequenced or neatly arranged alphabetically, — the logos is Feral & Un-Cageable, Reproductive & Lusty.

I have recently wondered how our language (the logos) would look/fare *without* the dictionary (void of reference). What would the "Unmoored" word (the Wild/Feral Logos) look like if it were free to roam, migrate, hybridize.

To view the *Inferential* replace the *Referential*.

---

5 *Melancholia: Hinge as Innominate Limina* (McNally Jackson, 2016) exemplifies a multi-teamed approach to densify the 'particle.' Not only are we employing multiple Modules, but we are also treating/investigating the term from multiple disciplines, i.e., Drawing, Essay, Criticism, Poetry. *Melancholia:* represents the second multi-participatory Hinge Event following *Hinge Trio* (La Alameda Press).

These comments initiate an ongoing exploration of Hinge Theory. But when asked to explain Hinge Theory, the proper response would be the same as to someone who asked you what the sky looks like, — you would usher them outside, point upward, & say "Look." Look, then, to the works themselves.

"Hinge By The Slice" first appeared in *Talisman* #46, 2018.

Further Reading

<u>The Books:</u>

Smelling Mary (Howling Dog Press)
from stone this running (Black Widow Press)
Wrack Lariat (Black Widow Press)
Hinge Trio (La Alameda Press)
Melancholia: Hinge as Innominate Limina (McNally Jackson)
tenebraed (Black Widow Press)

<u>The Interviews</u> (read chronologically):

"No Rust on These Hinges – A Heller Levinson Interview,"
   The Jivin' Ladybug
      https://jivinladybug.wordpress.com/2011/04/22/heller-levinson-interview/
"So Much Depends on the Hinge: Heller Levinson,"
   The Jivin' Ladybug
      https://jivinladybug.wordpress.com/.../so-much-depends-on-the-hinge-
      heller-levinson
"Ephesus Glom: An Interview with Heller Levinson, Part 1"
   by Jonathan Mulcahy-King, *X-Peri*, January, 2018
      https://x-peri.blogspot.com/2018/01/ephesus-glom-interview-with-
      heller.html?spref=fb

Reviews

"The Hinge Manual," Howling Dog Press
  https://issuu.com/howlingdogpress/docs/the_hinge_manual___related_
  criticism
"Smelling Mary" review by Leigh Herrick, *Jacket 38*, Late 2009
  jacketmagazine.com/38/r-levinson-rb-herrick.shtml
"tenebraed" review by Alison Ross, *Clockwise Cat Magazine*,
  2017
  http://clockwisecat.com/2017/04/1008/

Inquiries: hingetheory@gmail.com

Blade

forest fells wells ways   to[xiv]

par-take   summon issue

flame flesh flush-throughs

cutting edge to be on the... cut-ting edge [*leader*-ship] blade

as bloom garden forth from hand

handi-work

hand = the hinge enabling man to transition from an arboreal to

a bipedaling terrestrial creature

"The tool replaced the tree as man's chief object of prehension:

he went from gripping one kind of thing to gripping another,

both in the service of survival."[xv]

in the spurl-juice of enduring adjacencies

rotational contours

fit formation mutually modify[xvi]

from hand this blade

in the blade this handiwork

in the pith of a reoccurring hegemony

rail rally bluster pour   default ignite

    upcharge surcharge dismantle

the circle of fifths: dependable iteration

rarely hare the fallen. the wall of course. if fallen to inviolate

turn upright. measurement outweighs potential.

pilfer the mechanisms responsible probable cause the dearth of

destiny dark nights amid parity myths nullify monarchs faults

are disposable if you follow that ine of knobby rosarian hush

the pattern is not far off clatter g ng come the troops you could trip over come they so

surely so

full of cause

$2 + 2 = 4$

$6 + 2 = 3$

Well, why don't you Bo

Diddley me

in the pith of an ambulatory redux

fasicular cherish lurch unbundle righteous

em-bloom   en

jamb

counselling petrification: liquefy

flaneur waffle/   swizzle surge /   purl rustle

crewel

gloam

pearl pack knobs grassy gland vascular

bed

swathe

succulent

in the pith of a soft ember tap dance

emblematic of the turning is a

way toward. this too a way to.

    on pliable: metabolic

    on plausible: dare

    on fruit: fructuous

from postexilic obscurity the soothe-wardens converge

the long & short of it is corner luxuriance vertex croon the

sum of things

as always ambivalence is unhealthy

for the gums

in the pith of collapse

in the soot-swart maze of heterogeneous

knavery

      — maggot pilfer

      — tocsin revel

      — plunge putrescent unwind

purulent undermine

disturbance arrives as audacious un-do

unassured orthodoxies roach rattle

                        topple havoc demolition

decompose

'life' enshrouds life, dribbles ornamental

bonbons,

bandit-props nullify the pull-out,

the riptide quash, the

annihilative mow down

legitimacy hijacked

the heresy of

suspension

goes

unratified

in the char of a misplaced domesticity

carrion fettle   brim-burn   mandibular toxicity

burrowed deep the squall festers

m e t a s t a s i z e

irreverence parleys vituperation the

sting outweighs

moments of relevance battle for ointment

the 'seen' counterfeits the 'appearing'

will ambiguity ever qualify as sufficient definition

tooling a judicious proprietary

whispers

                like

spur

` ` ` ` ` ` ` ` ` `

we have been co-opted by the fleet

` ` ` ` ` ` ` ` ` ` `

Foucault: "When language arrives at its own edge, what it finds is not a positivity that contradicts it, but the void that will efface it. Into that void it must go, consenting to come undone in the rumbling, in the immediate negation of what it says, in a silence that is not the intimacy of a secret but a pure outside where words endlessly unravel."

` ` ` ` the *bes!erk* makes the application fashionable ~ ~ ~

reflecting on the alchemy of the module to catapult the particle

:: chambering the particle in the comfort of the module

provides the *nestle* necessary for emblazoned jaculation

how much of the

blues

is

meander

an agony

traipse

query in deliberative domain

speculation trumped the roundup flareful ardour pump

press evedentiary

        triste elopement

tertiary meld blend the velocities produce a sustainable sleep for

stone

undulant seas for piracy

what wild animal cankers the eye

query like collapsible fruit

meltdown   bunchings

            seed

serrying nonplussed pagodas pulsative trunk options expire

timelines skewer consideration mycelium directional monasticly

alert

seedfall   collapse enabling abandon

            abandon creating collapse

dissolution merriment

            ~   `   `   ~

there is in the resolve, often times, resolution

            ~~~~   ~   ~~~   ~

motility recovers from brokenness gets on. self-correcting is
cumbersome. entails pulling together. recovery. is time-sensi-
tive. of course this which is enterprise could be mistaken for
sloth or underdevelopment whereupon the lively inspired by
modification leaks a faulty sort of vintage catering to the archival
championing pause over attrition don't you know the code of the
cowboy is never to hurry.

whereofwith the replication excels the cantilever calypso when
you squawk go easy on the altitude upright is a privilege an
overview a stance scratching out a living pay heed grow what you
need why hands became so handy.

liking the way you put have to after the fact

this above all

summation   summaries

contributions as always a step back in time

it always comes down to: A). Feed

                          B). Transportation

                          C). Hermaphroditism

bearing the mean in mind can issue a reactionism severe rash –

clash clandestine – modified by churl adept remonstrance apos-

trophes in waiting rambunctious rock to roll forfeiture forgets

forgetting as corrupt erasure as reestablishment reestablishment

as penance shortcuts lead to fustigation a peculiar form of ro-

mance overshadows divisions schisms secularity hedonism the

influence of bad taste divides the dark dreary – *dread banks* –

plugged to puissance tailored suits depend upon time of day

clean sheets the cut of the swagger cost lively cut costly cost

corny cheer bravely administer breath breathe fully broach the

torch touch membrane tensile tongue tonsil tolerance

tender

lovely

evenings

{{ If you are not mystified,

You are not paying attention. }}

in the pith of pulse

purl cumulative

                                    pulsation : pulsative

                                                 : perturbation

where in

perturb

is impulse

division hive:

right ventricle/left ventricle

left atrium/right atrium

2 beat psadatephelomy[xvii]

fleet of the hind supple of the breast

catchall careen chaos crucifixion crossover crux

lolling in the Lilliput of love custodianship wears red

                                                                being

other than you were requires satisfaction roll in the hay playtime

in the Sierras the query perpetuates grain

the Winter of my horizon I saw you

I saw you

without so much as a start the wind felt shadow feel shadow

beside. bedside. epistolary wraith. writ large.

the imprint too

Q. What does that knife do that the other
   10 don't?

A. It goes with my corduroys.

in the denaturing of things[xviii]

regalia retch   rook retrograde

croon contagious acidic redden

no leaves on the trees

aqueducts torched corrosive quoit

huntsmen on the run

lug weary

the results are

in

The appaloosa nodded as if she understood. perhaps she did. it was not a woeful tale… neither was it joyful or uplifting. it hung in a balance. an oscillative twang. she fed as I watched,… eyed me as she chewed.

in the morning we rode off.

. nomadism: grooming the reflex

. a mystified meteorite

. criteria as a basis for rumination

. decipherability acquaints well with hedonism

. albeit & likewise

The Big Squeeze

Ocular Compression. the 20th century urban surge, wrought

iron, the the grid, the gird, the enshroud, the erection-*ality*. high

rise field vision blunt. blockade. the view-point *blindered*; the

out-look blasted.

eyes leashed to devices more & more miniaturized. — shrink

contagion —. the rangy, lopey, sensibility endangered.

flaneurism extinct. we dwell in the vision-stricted catacombs of

self-incarceration.

myopically doomed.

visually petrified.

in the pith of fulcrum

quintessentially   furnace fist

cupola burn   iron-hearted demises close to

sibilance horror-lit beside rogue currencies

pick & choose above all

the pattern

where in the

fulcrum fulminates

jointure rattle   disintegrate edge

lunar wallop

tide

gather

crux crewel   supplemental

        buffeting the surmise

at what point in the gathering does the collection become

assessable. how does criteria assemble. how does judgement

discharge.

the gathered travels

                    to qualify

as accumulation

where in the

accumulative

is enterprise

enterprise

initiation   instill   install[xix]

                                        [put into place

                                        [put in one's place

                                        [the hermeneutics of place

                                        placement

installment

enterprise begets installation

enter – 'go into'

prise – 'to lever open'

    go into open

   to open the open

. where does one go *to* in the open

. what part of open is clearance

. what part of clearance is elsewhere

push-back clears the way to open

                       to

*en-**trance*** into the place of open

Circumference dissolves into a generalized diffuse.

    — Essential Erasure —

    — Suspirant Interstitial Suffuse trance

lull-loll   lure   parallax

                                     gather

                                     harness/retain

to fall into a trance

to induce a trance

where in the

trance

is

linger

"A famous passage in the Mahabharata describes the testing of

Drona's pupils in archery. An artificial eagle has been prepared

by craftsmen and set up at the top of a tree to be a mark. Three

pupils are asked: 'What do you see?' and each answers: 'I see yourself, the tree and the eagle.' Drona exclaims: 'Away with you; these three will not be able to hit the mark;' and turning to Arjuna, 'the mark is for you to hit.' Arjuna stands stretching his bow, and Drona continues: 'Do you also see the tree, myself and the bird?" Arjuna replies: "I see only the bird.' 'And how do you see the bird?' I see its head, but not its body.' Drona delighted, says: 'Let fly.' Arjuna shoots, cuts off the head and brings it down."[xx]

peripheral fade ://: the identified magnified[xxi]

in the pith of fathom

core   correlative   conjoin

               conjunction

murk-embed → embellish

      depth delinquency

      fulcrum plunge

      flagella flagellate

from bounds this wobble intrench

shu(dd)(tt)ering through buttes of ordained frequencies

front-running jackhammer stench the telling & retelling girdle

cur-combed halls   pistil-mirth   feral-gesticulate

the outreach reels

rallying

adamantine

      :: the lodgings across tow 1 were more spacious. more

conducive to cohabitation. but v 10 would want to. ::

7/28/17

in the pith of an overwhelming meander

planeur-engffle   wallop-loop

dwic-do

parad?bling   c........   ....

8/1/17

vessel

sheath legacy   loll

blind
blinkage

room-los patter-ripple ....
wrench   shuttle   paradiddle   bob
no emphatic roll along

both water erupts
utensil
utensil or liquid
legacy-sheath

barrad

vessel →   hollow of concave
case →   a utensil
that lodgement
a shank legacy ....
a crate for travel
or water
snow white
modes
floatable

in the pith of an overwhelming meander

flaneur-waffle   wallop-lob   tensile-smooch

                    do-si-do

loom-lob patter-pizzle causeway retch wrench paradiddle

shuttle bob

where in the

drift[xxii]

is

tear

how much

        gathering

accumulates

from

drift

so much depends upon

conspicuity[xxiii]   →   *a-ppearing*

the appearing amasses in the accumulative

accumulation emboldens gather[xxiv]

the sweet-scented *hurl*

silences

the huntsman

Vessels

hinging Bonnie Lynch[xxv]

to travel   to

move along   *rim trotting*

: to fill [with water → vase

: to remove [firing removes water from clay

: to empty [withstand water → ship

pottery: crafted   as-sembled

the piety of parts

blush flotation

                      to hold ://: to cherish

firing clay from fragility… sintering transformative atomic

diffuse

— trip warden

— gland lard

where in the vessel is the hand

the ooze that moves along

in the pith of vast → trough-tread   vacancies va-

cillative   ,   aperture hollows   ,   up-shotted

the peer that registrates

— sheath legacies

sleuth motility

in the pith of loam

lambent meander   leafy larvae

                bellicosity purl

the stuff of walrus, lacinia, polyphonic madrigals, horsehair on

the bluff,… circumstantial

gotta be a fool to bluster forth like that   as if there were no

tomorrow   no providence   no reckoning

the gangbangers never considered you'd tadpole them in retalia-

tion stuff of dreams unruly canisters even bribes dismissed with

an adept symmetry how curious you didn't falter when compro-

mised so much muster

yet

in the pith of swarm

succulence   succor

        sluice-seethe

a bent

  direction

a common   al   ity

wrest-wallop → wrangler

      roustabout roundup

where in the swarm is rumination

the quiver-load ambulating

dissimulation

rend   at odds with

specifically the tear that dissembles

                                    . flees from…

dispatch   ornamentalizing the saccharine the

bloodhorn resounds   blasts

shun-guards   subterfuge   the equipage is faulty albeit the tanks

ruddy with heteroclite

feign-to   snarl   foil

trickster

the feint the dare derring-do dumpsters go lively go

unravel circulate pumpkin oil propositions plump the

plumbing goes unnoticed

goes

desuetude

rag picked   wrack dry   rook wrecked   rust fricative

wrench wobble

reel-ing

molding inutile

slake tongue spittle

fulsomely merrily roll along we rock roll roll relentless restless

roll on buddy meander stroll roil pearl pole pixilate percolate

perforate speculate ejaculate tabulate totter titter shameless

twitter tumble rumble bellicosity fumble firm glow seed game

ignite flame trounce tame glum garden glucose lame merrily

interpolate ambulate not too late move groove splice sail slice

dice go ooh la la go ooooooh

in the spear of annihilative

rack — ronin — rout — rumble

        . reincarnation

        . rustle

        . rustler

        . ruck

rust

reimbursement

arrears

in the blear of annihilative

Rotterdam.   den of thieves.

so much glory on mountain tops.

snowcapped.   solar shimmer

icicle drip

a nipple hardening

in the blear of an overwrought annihilative

smithereens smash crash lash ladies lassies asses drop passes

clambake curdle cuddle tousle blush muscle trample preamble

slash trash bash burn contain sustain retain retrain abstain

exhort abort exhort run d o

w n

spellbound

rebound

hellhound

the rigging uneven yet perpetual the wayfarer's pledge

from posit to positioning

averting betrayal I fulsomely. as in a whodunit. as if inquiry

alone could justify.

the ripening overt but symmetrical so one couldn't be too sure in the pith of a charred buoyancy

singe grapple grip rattle

scrubbed clean flammability courses a multidimensional

wherewithal

                                 intersects a rarefied bipedalism

                                 bewilders the necessity for overload

is abbreviation abortive

constituencies threaten to cavil

the landlocked suffer lockdown

the challenges for formalism are

all inclusive

saunter

the stretch that capitalizes

. accumulative allowance

. aperture hoist

cobbling discernments discretion seizes

lolling with bell tones

gloam glisten disarm

the satisfactory dissatisfied

deprived of

ruminative bareback groin epiphanic spine straddle

where in the

straddle

is

recourse

the gift that undulates

the williwaw that salutes

smelling saunter

edelweiss   pine nut   cedar

            falafel

in the pith of a fiberglass perfidy

pungency   cauliflower

        verdigris

fathom

plunge plum plummet

                — fetch plume

an errand gone stray   far afield

falling

percolative

linger

loose n   s   p   r   e   a   d

lessen   (mitigate, draw down, downsize, miniaturize – to squeeze through
       (aperture), to de-spatialize to populate, amplify opening, to 'knead' through

let go

un

burden

l   i   q   u   i   f   y

                                                        [where in the
                                                          liquefaction
                                                          is
                                                          identity

disseminate rattle componential swell   *ensorcell*

soothe source re-source

meander

mull

"The hooves of our Mongol horses go everywhere,

They climb to the heaven and plunge to the sea."

 – Yulü Chucai, 1236

sear sinuosity soar   plunge peril

how much of

hoof

is in the

bow[xxvi]

fleet polish

zephyrean transfer

pulsative tangle

in the sylph-soused rouse-riddled year (1210) of the horse →

blunt perdition

steppe assault

court the wend-river-wrest-round-wrangle panaerobic plinth

conjunction

The Poetry Reading

is an opportunity for those smitten with insignificance to believe

otherwise.

stray

off course   deviate   (de-fiance) (de-finance ⊠ funnel off)
                                                    loafe

                    dissolve

                    absolve

errancy   the sanity of deviation   the sanctity of curse

                                                   the curse of sanctity

luff-waffle   path-wobble   sway astride

circulate eviscerate

way-less

displace ://: displease ://: appease

void succulence

slight-ing

boisterous in the schoolyard they got what was coming the yelp

never far behind but lanky in the lurk stricken stride strum the

thrum slowly glisten glide girdle glow grumble

growl

roam

gloam

varsity throughout

stroll through the saunter hop

but only for instance the tether in rampage in transit the promo-

tion-minded desist a remark cottoned set aside bundled heated

to a deliberate temperature delicacies skewed lopped in rangy

fashion suggesting

just suppose

smell was everything. he could whiff them out from a block

away. few made the cut.

the qualifiers were especially

to choose as offspring the curve not even unless contemplated

with short circuits assembly formation pittance pontoon possi-

bly a contravene plausible if issued pleasantly so little remains of

preciosity

with trickles everywhere catching up remains an art the

celebration which celebrates celebrities withstanding those

nothing mores with no furthers with further as the uncountable

countable

insert into a bowl of hot chocolate

stroll

ambulate   stir   larkspur   rustle-lob

                                   lop-troll

                                   loll-thistle

                                   trophy-strophe

blousy bluebells billow   broth borealis

sizzle-souse

meander swizzle

succulent surrender

notwithstanding

the weapons were inadequate the weather foreboding morale at

a low furtherly ebbing the odds luminous the catfish stinky peril

a point of view

the more the seemingly appears as the appearing the less

conviction is enterprise

momentum: temperature bleeding conspicuity

ambulatory

shift   stroll-ladle^{xxvii}

          list-girdle

round   round & round

               ruckus

               rustle

accumulate

hoist lariat reign, — rein-in   resin

                                                                     raisin

                                                                     resonate

the bring-to shivers in the ho(i)st of deposit   the wounded

carousel, the farrier leaves so much behind

agglutinateaggregateagglomerateacqui *si tion*   *aggra va tion*

the earliest dispatches inspired by hair in the teeth upon wither-

ing founded an empire boasting of free-for-all in the land of the

catch-all the umpire turned a blind eye

who pays for this?

$$R\alpha\beta - 1\,2\,Rg\alpha\beta = 8\pi T\alpha\beta.$$

accumulation oppresses aperture

weighs burden down clog clot gluts transparencies garrotes phi-

lanthropy encumbers trill

. to capture the moment

. is capturing a moment possible

. is capture momentous

[where in

the spool

lurks

fasten

Mr. H huffed he was overwhelmed consumed harried by trivials dwarfed by customaries hurried off to acquaint himself with himself before the auctioneers grew unruly.

S felt she could offer solace to Mr. H. could let some air out of his tires. industrious & sympathetic S was relentless in her endeavor. time was a knot a twist of opportunities advances regressions hopes disappointments hankerings,… the solution was not far from the res-olution,… the given a shorn upon.

Mr. H took it all in. in good fashion. it could be said Mr. H grew more soothe while S more animated.

peeling the evaporate

congregations implausible agencies turbulent a time of year con-

venient for grief,... occasionals, fitful, frost, flammability, cus-

tomized flirtations, subject matter squashed workshops

suffocate pile-ups pile heap heapfully if you're troubled by this

right-so in a comprehensibility independent of claims, proce-

dures, oversights, boasts of "I'm on the board ..." tragic bleeds

the turnstiles pumps pollution pullulate poison Sammy On The

Run varnish the vanish just so looks good disdain discolors way-

ward pouts a squandered meander dubious sonorities rickety rot

pustulate pittances shrunk leather splatter deformables pray to

prey to

Burroughs said "the way in is the way out"

were it

so

where in

                                        the

evaporative

          is   the

constable

dog walkers in NYC amount to an underground system

fulsomely cheerily the rock the stone the whole stew

                                        bit by bit

                                        sparse   parcel

bundle without ties

tie subversion?

as in the game is tied

neutralized bound?

dumbbells make a difference

fulsomely wholesomely the whole merrily

we stroll[xxviii] along

insubordination pays a price

flame dragging the geodesic precession[xxix] spur hive spelunkers

spurt splendiferous squirt blossoms plunder perilous hard-

charging bear on fire juju herbs spiral slip slog swill galoshes

sumptuousity pinwheels clear the table win the bet

speaking of love much to speak of; speak:

to strip "love" of its loveliness; to make it more *use-ful*. In Peter

Hanke's, *The Moravian Night*, the protagonist "believed more in

mutual enthusiasm than in love, or at least he avoided using

the word."

To root around for a word more precise, less generically

neutered, less scrubbed clean of cogency – i.e., "I love you, I love

you too" —, less knee-jerk reflex & more revelation. "Mutual enthusiasm," however, lacks heft. Does love vanish or lessen in degree when enthusiasm wanes? A term with more all-encompassing ardor, a "wrap" for all seasons pleads to come forth. Alternates: *Retrofitting Affliction; Valvular Elation; Gilded Approximation; Crusted Contraction, Exquisite Thermals….*

This is an area of ongoing investigation.

<< perplexion is the root of invention >>

in the pith of aptness

aptitude   application   appropriate

apportionality

co-conspirators in the hierarchy of aces

appurtenance

: trilling the rim-shot bumptious borealis burgundy broth

incandescent Oompa Loompas rattle crank griddle cattle gear to

market to go deaf thataway :

this that that, that, most of all

piercing vacuum

klunk'a whambam chiaroslam

    flush phantasm spore

itinerant misfit   adjacency plight

mermaid meet might merrily

plot contrar over ily red runnin river run root roast roost curl

    perforate   confabulate   incarcerate

        industrialize   mobilize

in the assembly of parts the gap speaks

    seep-sultry

the wren of atmosphere

the tale of winds un

ordinanced

Maximizing the Hygiene of Disarray

disjoint

disjoin

disorient

douse

diligence

linger

loosen   s   p   r   e   a   d

lesson

let go

un-burden

relativity release relinquish runrunrun   roustabout askew

slantwise   out of kilter   *til*-ted

          trunk space   fit   fit for   fitting *in*

flummox flimsy flint

                    — foil

measurement   cherish instrumentalizes

care   ("to know, know, know you,/ is to love, love, love you,/ and

I do, yes, I do, yes, I do")

                    colossal aptitude

                    luff awry

                    snugless in the robust untether

meander to abandon,

          scatter roam unstitch loose vast anti-combinatorial

panoplies whirl to the one-eyed rhumba jabberwocky patch to

the dazzle of hypnotic mesmeric *tanoura* spray trammel to rum

buffoonery lurch to the cosmic unlatch

askew in vexative disarray

disqualified from the marching band

topsy-turvy trombone drool

reveille with ill-fitting trousers

reliability depends upon premature remorse

a bug in the hand beats a bite on the skin

tumbleweed   tactility   orthogonal

the one missing glove made for a cold hand

so much

so kind

so what

the New York Sky dribbles the smell of eucalyptus

the rubber ball purses the youth

elsewhere there is sound

consider : to consider : consideration

to mel(d)(t) mould into the tempo of merge

      . the inclination that disposes

      . rum disguise

      . consider conjugating conjuration

to be a → Mist Embezzler

      → Vaporous Masher

trampling the causeway to fuddle with misfits peppered

apoplectic minerality lodges

a knobby perturbation void of loin

loss

degradation

pitted

an en

suing

empty

Concerning HL/LL Intercourses:

The Intercourses do not distinguish themselves by responding to, commenting/narrating upon, or ornamentalizing. Unlike what is termed Ekphrastic poetry which usually reflects the traits above, the Intercourses *fuse-with* or *fuse-Into* a compounding magnification where each is both a part of & wholly one another. The action could be described as a porous absorption drizzling from a Hovering Oscillative.

What is it to draw (the 'draw' applying equally to the lingual) if the drawn-forth fails to appear as the 'drawn.' The 'drawn' here being that which is fully fleshed out, that which has developed as a 'draw-ing.' For text & drawing to develop as the *underdeveloped* requires threshold-hopping, a continuous solicitation to ignite the 'hidden' without obscuring its 'hiddenness'. A peek-a-boo

preceding an evaporative, a presentation featuring Phantom

Reverberation.

Karst

volatility-lash   squa(ll)wk-swell

        rattle-udd(tt)er

parcel array tributarial teem

        rock rambunction

        quell rake

warp-wrought-serendipitous ungulate wrack

            sere sieve sleave pack

conjugate tremor

collectivize lure

                                clump gristle

                                gourd-gizzard

from what bellows-frost .. *this* ..

across what blear belch-gardens these ampouled abecedaria

drizzle-pour   drench-drain   drumlord

               word waggle

pebbling the blazing perspicuity of skull

          beleaguer

          stir

          roughshod

          rustle-quirk

          quiddity

fulminate   precedent

through the unstrained archipelago of rare lucubrations

fur-tumble sessile-lunge the ravening intrepid clench-gorge con-

summates subterranean gouge

outreach connubiates upbringing

bell wobble wallop storm

cling   dislodgement

pulp

palpi

tation

in the mucous of antediluvian mist

eer i ly   war i ly   dunness   a

crawl space   larkspur loop throttle

divinations unapproachable by glass

            a complicit transparency

where shadow parlays shadow

where accumulations

        like calico

        like breath

suckle

moss

sibyl

lips

loon-lob

circulating a species
of gerata...

compacted
catapults
trebuchets
mangonels

Onon River
Burkhan khaldun - sacred
mountain

lobt-lopping

cuneiform

oneiric   talon spray

wind whipped

volatilized

sluice slather

sulde[xxx]

"Laddering Capillarial in the Great Embark." Mongolian Shaman

hoof/shaft/blade/— horsehair-hefted → circulating a species

aeration, stallion volatilized, the seer-slather slumber-rattle of an

archaic genuflect shudders Burkhan Khaldun[xxxi] with the heave

of a thunderous trebuchet

larded with ventillative dispatch radiating quaquarversal em-

anates stitched to a hooded adumbrative, runic

tufts transmute, collect, … disperse,

wind-whip talismanic talon spray →

                loon-lop   loft-list

         lattice-wind   wizzle-lob

strained through cabalistic ethers galloping teleportative hitched

to the sear of an enduring emblazon in the lop-lobbing journey beyond dynasties & dithyrambs

in the pitch of a non-conjectural asymptomatic destiny

the brood

unbraids

in the underfolds of an advanced logomachy

serried rudder flap breeze-blight transparencies lop the filigree

silt-stifled coronas insure effulgence a moribundity…

abbreviations the rub, voltaic rob, cauterizers campaign, promote

vesicular atrophy, throttled esophagus,

in the bloat of suffocative char leech-lordships grounded in gar-

rote sizzle non-redeemable strychnine over a shrank shrivelliza-

tion, a

shrunk endeavor

how much of

currency

is

reissue

indefatigably the lure of undulate seethes from ghost shroud

jalopies through winds with invisible fire updraft sickles the stall perspires oscillative in the lurk of the hidden sessile seared surge

solar spurred jangle driven modals concatenate the undercurrent

hurl

unblemished nascencies…

perplexed

joyous

this, then this too

this then, this too

this then this too

Ephesus Glom:
An Interview with Heller Levinson, Part 1

by Jonathan Mulcahy-King

Jan 2018

Proscenium

Ephesus was the birthplace of Heraclitus, the pre-Socratic Ionian thinker who abdicated Apollonian rigidity for flux, the essence of his universe. As a first scientist, in the western sense, this marked an important turning-away from ontology to a more expressive, linguistically challenging mode of inquiry. *Glom,* as in to clutch, to grasp, to secure. Enter self-proclaimed hinge scientist, Heller Levinson, author of six books of practice-led research exploring "Hinge Theory:" *Smelling Mary* (Howling Dog Press, 2008), *From Stone This Running* (Black Widow Press, 2011), *Hinge Trio* with Linda Lynch and Felino A. Soriano (La Alameda Press, 2012), *Wrack Lariat* (Black Widow Press, 2015), *Melancholia: Hinge As Innominate Limina* with Will Alexander, Mary Newell, and Linda Lynch (McNally Jackson Books, 2016) and *Tenebraed* (Black Widow

Press, 2017). As the above would suggest, Levinson has adopted the modus operandi of capturing flux, holding the flow, embracing the liminality of language. *X-Peri* interviews Heller in anticipation of his new book *LinguaQuake* (forthcoming in February from Black Widow Press), the latest installment of hinge theory in practice, an important and exciting offering in an otherwise emptyful deluge of form. Contributor to hinge theory, Mary Newell, has defined Hinge as a '… material of connectivity that introduces an intentional and generative biasing'. Michael Annis', author of the *Hinge Manual*, has reinforced Hinge Theory by citing the 18th century German philologist Jacob Grimm, noting that hinge merely follows the various sound variables, morphemes etc. already inherent in the make-up of language. Elsewhere, Grace Dane Mazur in her anthropological studies of Lascaux, Renaissance and Byzantine images[1] relays the idea that hinges work to highlight the entrancing lure of various real and metaphysical thresholds. Catherine Barnett describes "hinge words" as allowing the poet both '… continuity and gap; unity and difference' and that "hinges" '… keep the parts of the poem in some working relationship to one another and at the same time allow the poem to retain some of what Aristotle calls the unities of time and place (Taken from 'A Brief Poetics of the Hinge.'[2]) Enter Heller Levinson, Hinge functions more as a type of counter-language than a vehicle for ideas, it is the freshly laid highway, the sound of a hidden river, bringing hope and ideas of infrastructure to tired settlers——it is the wormhole.

Jonathan: Welcome, Heller! Thanks again for taking the time to riff with *X-Peri,* as always we are very excited to have you! Off the bat, could you describe for readers (or 'un-describe') the key tenets of this ambitious project/way of saying, referred to as "Hinge Theory"?

Heller: Even to "un-describe" would suggest that there is a structure to describe, which would be misleading. Instead of a list of tenets, I can suggest a foundational 'creed', which is that Language is alive (whether referring to organic or inorganic life would be another discussion), respirative & reproductive.

Hinge both molds & melts, is diffusive, emanative, disseminative, & collectivizing. It is the bird of prey & the swallow on the wrist. It is Revolutionary Liquidity immune to the Trump wall or the Clintonian fence.

Jonathan: As a creed then, hinge must be identifiable within a greater tradition, how would you situate hinge (its context, emergence, trajectory etc.) within the history of innovative poetry and poetics/linguistics? For me, it seems to be both a continuation and a criticism of L=A=N=G=U=A=G=E poetry, insofar as it concedes the ephemerality between beginnings and endings, while also challenging the principle that 'series is not essence', or is series too reductive here, as this might, in a sense, impinge on the flow of language hinge is attempting to amplify?

Heller: These are interesting questions as they highlight the difficulty of discussing Hinge in historical terms. As I have said before: "Hinge departs from all other poetic fashionings in declaring itself an ongoing ever-fulfilling linguistic enterprise." Hinge overlaps with any poetry that respects the integrity of Language as event, where the words of, say Gertrude Stein or Jackson Mac Low, create their own sculptural resonance. But, Hinge is definitively Not 'word salad,' a mix-mash of unlikely juxtapositions tossed together — mere gimmicky gamesmanship. Nor is it "I"—based personal narrative, which is as dead as the Image. Doctor Newell put it this way: "Hinge is material of connectivity and introduces an intentional and generative biasing. Like a pool table with all the balls commotioning and someone lifting the pool table slightly so all that activity is directed. (With the additional image that new balls are being added all the time as the pool table itself enlarges)."

At this point I would be fine with disengaging Hinge from any poetic context as it has so little resemblance to what is, in general, being practiced. It is my belief that Hinge is an under-recognized Universal Function that has 'emerged,' for those of us who are discussing it, in the format of language. There is no reason to believe that the same behaviorisms don't underlie botany, physics, mathematics, basketball, military science, etc. When discussing Hinge with a friend in the Special Forces he responded with: "Sounds like a multiplicitous simultaneous ambush."

Jonathan: So hinge is very much staked out in terms of forward-motion, it is both reactionary and incendiary, an interconnectedness inviting continuous work that can have more poems or 'modules' added to any one idea. Are there any new hinge developments you are aware of?

Heller: Yes. I have currently identified a new Hinge contribution: The Investigation of the Linguistically Undocumented. By this I mean words or ideas, which I am calling "terms"[3] that have been Under-Examined. I stumbled upon this insight while writing "tenebraed to trespass." Seeking to enrich my understanding of "trespass," I found the only resource I had to consult was my former work.[4] Exploring trespass led to an outcrop of terms such as *swarm, stroll, meander, aperture, ambulate, wander, drift, drip, seep, …* terms I had hinged previously. These shade-offs of the term being scrutinized, which in turn become scrutinized, form a Bundle of Constellative Refractive Impregnations. This behavior leads to a thickening of the Word, a greater musculature, & affords one a deeper intimacy than the current tendency toward pan-abbreviation. We employ Language to *Deploy* insight. A new universe materializes. The formerly abstract & remote is now Resplendently close-at-hand, — shoulder rubbing. Going back to your mention of the "language school" where cleverness reigns, this is a stark departure. The applications[5] are very clearly mission oriented, methodically conducted, an archaeology intent upon di(g)scovery. Comments about there is 'nothing left to be done' in the arts is laughable when one perceives the sheer overload of opportunity just 'begging for it.' In the upcoming volume, *LinguaQuake*, terms such as *aptness, askew, knot, vacancy* are being addressed/investigated & disseminate other terms which in turn will be applicated & cycle back to densify/magnify the original term. I hope this discussion stimulates some activity in this area of the *remote approachable.*

Jonathan: Reinterpretation plays a large role in what you are saying, there is an almost beat-like philology at play here (previously in interviews you have replaced the word "collaboration" with the word "intercourse" as a way of better expressing the intentions present (or missing) from everyday language, and in the case of the latter... the sheer 'fucky'-ness of it). This gives a wider sense of what we could otherwise think of as "momentum language", made up of the gerundial, appropriate sound making and association. How much of hinge would you say is hermeneutics?

Heller: I would be more comfortable with saying multiple submissions or offerings rather than 'reinterpretation,' as that might suggest a devaluing of the original application. A comparison might be to Cézanne's 82 paintings of Monte Sainte-Victoire, a mountain he studied at differing times of day from varying perspectives, a 'motif' undergoing ongoing scrutiny.

One must resist the temptation to enclose (circumscribe) the newly emerging within the already existing, i.e., hermeneutics. Such tendencies sacrifice 'novelty' to the safety nets of the familiar. I appreciate the Philosophical Hermeneutics of both Heidegger & Hans-Gadamer.[6] I very much like the way they attempt to dethrone the subject, to fore-play/cleanse the foreground, the eidetic reduction permitting 'otherness' to appear. Similarly, Hinge is opposed to the Western white man's rectilinear hubristic notion of ego/subject as supreme leader, — the idea that whether conscious or unconscious the self is always choosing. Hinge suggests ego dissolution through Linguistic-Fusion as one approach. The Hinger becomes an element among elements, an instrument among instruments. At this level of creation, each word insists on its word associates. The practice is to detect the reproductive impulses inherent in the word being witnessed. The 'you' is no longer choosing the word or the syntax, it is the 'life' of the word fulfilling its own path. 'You' as no longer a domineering filtration system, but an absorptive, contiguous, cohabitation. As we are developing an aptitude for animal intelligence & the sensate of trees, let us also sensitize to the ecology of language. The calling is to 'uncover,'[7] to approximate the mysteriously elusive.

I trust ignorance, i.e., I don't have a clue how this experience or that experience led to the experience or expression in question, unless I am approaching a piece on the Mongolian Eagle, or the Native American Indian, as in "from Buffalo this Indian,"[8] — these applications are direct results of study & examination, stimulus & response.

> *Hinge was not manufactured, it was*
> *discovered, & continues in that vein*
> *of wonder & enterprise.*

Jonathan: I took two classes on Heidegger's *Being And Time* as an undergrad, part 1 & 2, the professor was a philologist writing a new translation, you could tell it consumed him as he dove into every reassigned word, every piece of jargon, it became so abstract I feel like I know Heidegger as I know Joyce or Thomas, or Heller Levinson for that matter. Also, that's a great point about premature labelling; new ideas need time to breathe. You're right also in that a lot of emphasis gets put on the cultural-intuitive links we make when writing, again, this is all about personal responsibility and author/ownership (see our above exchange re. c-words). Are there any limitations or so-called limitations you have encountered working with Hinge?

Heller: No.

Jonathan: How self-regulated is the work in practice, could we for example, hinge together other peoples' work? Also, there is a strong influence of musicality in the work and in your reading practice, though presumably hinge need not rely on externalities or given 'lyrical' clichés? How important is the beat?

Heller: Absolutely. One work can Hinge to another work. It can also mix-mash-cutup & copulate with other work. Hinge is intended to invite inclusivity so that 'terms' can receive the full exuberance benefiting from multiple inquiries. My intercourses with the visual artist, Linda Lynch, exemplify this. We Hinge to a term such as Pathos stimulating expansion, complementarity, & densification, which enriches the lifeblood of "Pathos." In the case of Hinging to a drawing such as Linda's "Karst Drawing," I fructify a double Magnification, — thickening the term as well as Linda's drawing exploring the term. I have also hinged with musicians such as the guitarist, Joe Giglio, saxophonists Jimmy Halperin, & Sedric Choukroun.[9] Now that we're on the topic I must revisit your question "are there any limitations I have encountered" & reverse my former response with an emphatic Yes. I lust to work with a dancer or dance company, to explore how they could further flesh-out the terms. I would love to work with mathematicians, architects, physicists, & other disciplines. Living a life dedicated to exploring infinitudes, I am limited by my finitude.

Music/beat are quintessential. If I assert that 'language is alive,' then certainly it is both rhythmic & musical. Language is Juicy with Sound. At my last reading I had the audience sing-out a line with me – *"pothole ruckus backwater bushwhack."*[10] If one recites the line from the belly, with full breath, recites the line with gusto, puts one's whole body into it, relishing the fleshiness of the words on the lips, the vibrations of the embouchure, the result is deLiCious. I call it a word-tasting.

Jonathan: Very interesting, I would love to see you hinge with an architect! Though I suppose it would be easier at technical drawing or model stage, still, the possibilities are endless! I hope like Gaudi or Hundertwasser, you might one day have your very own "hinge village" somewhere in the mountains! This is very ambitious for a poet; it actually reminds me a lot of Joseph Beuys, when he introduces the idea of social sculpture into his philosophy of art. He too of course strove to escape categorization, to open up new possibilities for what constitutes art practice.

Jonathan: Might the difficulty of language to which you are referring hint at a wider problem—that our propensity to extrapolate meaning in matters of experimental/innovative language is symptomatic of Wittgenstein's "language games", or a rule-governed character of analysis that feeds our auto-effective desire for meaning? How might this relate to your work, and how might we better discuss "meaninglessness" in innovative poetry practice?

Heller: Yes, there is a wider problem, & it is the nullification in the post-Sumerian[11] world of a vitalistic, open-ranging, un-bordered, inclusively responsive uncaged virility. To a large extent, the 'blinders' are a result of commercialization. Commercialism has necessitated indexing, record keeping, filing, labeling, shelving, categorization, packaging, coupled with the necessity to attract consumers. Consumers want it neat & tidy, shiny & glazed, easily digestible. This is the transactional world & may be necessary to manage the working day. But it does not address the interior life of the individual. Clearly these impulses are contaminating poetry & can readily be seen in the Academies reaping profit from MFA's, writing programs & the like. To attract students you need clear-cut course-definitions. You need to be able to talk about 'stuff.' Have you seen any course offerings for *Bafflement 101*? I would argue to leave a reader in a state of 'bafflement' should be considered an achievement. I urge legitimate poets to flee the schools & seek the uncomfortably undesignated.

Meaning as customarily approached insists on finality, on conclusion, on establishing. As you know, Hinge insists upon the ongoing & extensive. "Ongoing" does Not refer to a sequence, or from a start to a finish,[12] but more in the manner of leaping, associating,… Fecundating Rotational Clusters. I am very much enchanted by burrowing into the *undeclared*. It is ironic that in this time of technological tyranny & GPS locatability the modern soul has never been more lost, more anguished. In America, suicides are up & the number of persons on opioids is steadily rising.

How does our idea of "meaning" fare against our notion of the "Glimpsed?" A glimpse would be difficult to transform into 'meaning' because it asserts itself as insufficient. Yet the 'glimpse' beckons us, urges us to *take-in* more (*the augmentative peer*) — "the regard is the look strapped with the interrogative."[13] Perhaps we are closer now to your last question: "How might we better discuss 'meaninglessness' in poetry?" If you look at many of my titles such as *the road to lost road, trespass in cumulative bruise, tenebraed to a capsizing algorithm, tenebraed to nothing*, you can see that I am searching for insights that dwell where 'meaning' abdicates. Could we not say something like this: Hinge seeks to explore nutrition where meaning has no meaning. Or, instead of saying 'meaningless,' let's propose that we seek insights that mean something other than what meaning means, not meaningless, simply *Other-li-ness*.

Recently I have become fascinated by the notion of facets, aspects of things, those splinters ('Splinter' is investigated in the upcoming *LinguaQuake* — "the Splinter in its disengagement flares into the Open") that assert they are not an entirety, that cannot be checked-out at the register, — the realm of the non-scannable.

Jonathan: Yes, bafflement! The Nietzschean blow to the temples, the disjointedness we need to see beyond our given pinhole. I also agree with your comments concerning a need for categorisation, as belonging to a particular tradition of inquiry "… just throw it in the [Dada] box and move on". However, commercialism, consumerism and more generally, capitalism, are enabled by the coveting of copyright (that's a lot of "c-words"!) Equally, innovation, in striving to be so asymptotic (in an anti-commercial sense), might also rely too heavily on the above processes you mention, suffering the same nullifying fate in the name of over-inventiveness. For example, we might ask why it is many innovators are so averse to playing with cliché, it seems still too hot to pick up and toss around. Do you think cliché will "cool" anytime soon?

Heller: I cannot speak for what others are averse to or not & I don't follow the current stock value of cliché. Personally, I think cliché can serve as a challenge to revitalize something that has become stale. A word such as "gossamer" should be resuscitated. I would welcome a book entitled *Cliché* where the formerly ghettoized would appear as the newly freed. "Bring-it-on" so to speak. For the record, I see Hinge as being not so much about 'innovating' as 'reclaiming,' – restoring language to the firmament of its original fire & gases.

Jonathan: Finally then, my closing question is in the form of a poem on a key theme in our discussion, what could be considered "the tragicomedy of backward turning."

Feb. 1916 – Mar. 1915

Avenger na dna Victim A><
tnevloS A *Type <blockquote>*
bannock bread baking in ice
auger holes, hesperian flight-
ripped aluminium slopes </
–A Test* <a*
renepO eyE nA *Source</a> *
– saedi desserper rof evlav ytefas
Wisdom and for folly }×¨˜ï»Ì
snoitpecnocerP fo noitageN A
<hr color="#FF0000"> – feileR A
dellud nehw – tnalumits A
Amb(ush)ition of a poet
*</blockquote>*uterus deiraew nehw – tser A
– noitnevnoC dna msilaicremmoC
iti ishki (cut-off, lost): drawn to the zenithal
lure</gurglingrush</ brown bottles bobbing
despite the pulling dregs of Palaeolithic lake
lethargic ghost-dance *<blockquote>*
fo saes gnitteseb eht ni ecnednepedni
gnirudne fo telsI ydruts A
– modeerf laer fo sisao nA *href="http://www.pewarts.org/9/*
samplemain.html" target="_blank">Online
but the reproductive power. Mixer susurrus:
selfhood phenylmethane sellenders not unmucilaged?

Heller:

trespass   falter   linger

        en

        dure

how much of

linger

is

fascination

... the template exceeds the interim ...

1   See *Hinges: Meditations on the Portals of the Imagination*, AK Peters/CRC Press.

2   The University of Arizona Poetry Center.

3   When a term is chambered in a Hinge Module it has been called the 'particle.' At this point particle/term/subject matter can be viewed as interchangeable. See "Hinge Diagnostic", *Smelling Mary*, p.71

4   See "with trespass," *Smelling Mary*, p.113; "trespass in obdurate credulity," "trespass like rolling liquidity," "trespass in cumulative bruise, among others, *From Stone This Running*, pp. 191, 193, 194.

5   The 'application' or 'postulate' replace the term 'poem'

6   In *ToxiCity*, pp. 102, 103, 104, three applications are devoted to "Contouring Philosophical Hermeneutics: "The Expressed Expresses The Inability To State What Is Said In The Unsaid;" "The Expressed Inability Expresses The State To What In The Unsaid Said Is;" "In The What Is Said The Unsaid Expresses To The Expressed State Inability."

7   The Greek word for truth is "Alethea" which translates as – unhiddenness.

8   *Wrack Lariat*, p. 163

9   See "part beatitude/part beast," YouTube.

10 from "the road to melancholy road," in *Melancholia As Innominate Limina*, p. 93

11 See *Apocalypse*, D. H. Lawrence, Penguin Books.

12 A future exploration of the term "glide" beckons.

13 *Wrack Lariat*, p. 205.

Jonathan Mulcahy-King is the author of *Euryphion* (Ed du Cygne; X-Peri Series, 2017), Editor-in-Chief of *The Licentiam* and Assistant Editor of *X-Peri*. He hails from Newport, South Wales.

Spray

The following edifications supplant "Endnotes" with "Spray" to suggest irrigation through drifting back to the motifs, much as a fine mist recirculates to sea after the crash of a large wave. This elevates elucidations from formalistic sequestration to a more nimble, interosculative 'cast-back.'

Spraynotes

i   Emily Dickinson writes, "tis like the Distance/On the look of Death," Ponder: the 'Distance' on the look of Life, on the skin of an apple, on peels of laughter, on fade, … florescence. (see 'tenebraed to distance,' page 20).

ii   According to James L. Brooke, "agriculture and land clearance have played a major warming role. Land that is cleared of forest, often through burning, emits huge amounts of CO_2 as does the annual plowing and harrowing of soil. But agriculture also contributes huge amounts of methane to the atmosphere, either from cattle digestive systems or emissions from rice paddies, essentially artificial wetlands, which are also a source of natural methane emissions." (*Climate Change and the Course of World History*, 477).

iii   Much of the material on Nitrogen was stimulated by Robert B. Marks's discussion of the Nitrogen Cycle in his book, *The Origins of the Modern World* (Roman & Littlefield, 2015).

iv   "It would not be a matter of 'giving speech back' to animals but perhaps acceding to a thinking … that thinks the absence of the name as something other than a privation." Jacques Derrida, "The Animal That Therefore I Am." We are seeking to explore where in the unspoken, spoken Is, and, where in the spoken lurks the 'unsaid.' See Heller Levinson, "Contouring Philosophical Hermeneutics" in *Toxicity* (Howling Dog Press, 2005).

v   See *ToxiCity*, p.102

vi   We will be identifying words (in this case: 'splinter') as Hinge Operatives (hereafter referred to as HO). Our mission is to explore these Under-Examined (to 'operate' them) in the hopes of releasing their Luciferous Indigenity. To densify them with Original Significance.

    A.   Including "splinter" in the repertoire of Hinge Activities adds dimension & texture to behaviorisms such as: 'import/export,' 'migratories,' 'modular collapse', etc.; to view a migratory as a splintering thickens our notion of how a migratory behaves. We might also en-vision a 'peel,' a 'shave-off,' a 'slip,' a 'slide,' currently words under consideration.

B. How does the identity of the "thing-splintered-from" alter? How repairs the splintered-from?

C. "For Freud, when the thing splinters and loses its identity, the word is still there to restore that identity or invent a new one. Freud counted on the word to reestablish a unity no longer found in things." The 'word' in this context would be guilty of Linguistic Deceit. Hinge's labor to dismember the Signifier is an attempt to Restore Linguistic Integrity.

vii The impulse now is to "mine" (see *tenebraed*, p.16) "tenebraed to parting" (*tenebraed*, p.121) to flesh-out insights into the lesions, flexions, & facets of the splinter's 'parting-from'. facet-rumble mayhem churn chisel cheek burn

viii The Rilkean 'open' is visualized here as treated in The Eighth Elegy.

ix The energy of 'prying' as a crowbar might be used as leverage to open nailed wooden crates superpositions with Hinge.

A. Thinking here of quantum superposition which states that "much like waves in classical physics, any two (or more) quantum states can be added together (superposed) and the result will be another valid quantum state; and conversely, that every quantum state can be represented as a sum of two or more distinct states.

B. Unloading Hinge from physics terminology (where parallels can be dicey: "One must resist the temptation to enclose (circumscribe) the newly emerging with the already existing. Such tendencies will sacrifice 'novelty' to the safety nets of the familiar."(HL) we initiate a new Hinge term referring to correlative yet distinct activities as an En-Mesh.

x This is a significant modular shift from "the road to _____ road" (the "trail" as opposed to the "road") & represents a clash between the man-made, the Anthropocene, & the natural world. The difference between driving your vehicle to the supermarket for provisions & using your own legs (or animal power) to track down the trail of mule deer, caribou, or buffalo, for example.

xi "To find the animals that are willing to be killed, Dunne-za hunters travel along trails that reveal themselves in dreams." "Dreaming is the mind's way of combining and using more information than the conscious mind can hold." Hugh Brody, *The Other Side of Eden* (North Point Press, New York, 2000), 127.

xii   The building of the Three Gorges Dam by the Chinese on the Yangtze River (begun 1992) displaced more than 1 million people and endangered hundreds of species. It seems that the dam directly caused the extinction of the Chinese river dolphin.

xiii   See "smock blue," *Wrack Lariat* (Black Widow Press), 237.

xiv   See "with blade this into," p.133; "from sharpening this edge," p.47; "in the age of edged weapons," p.57; *from stone this running* (Black Widow Press, 2011). "Blade" employs facets of "Import / Export / Mine discussed in *tenebraed* (Black Widow Press), 15, 16, 17.

xv   *Prehension: The hand and the Emergence of Humanity* by Colin McGinn (The MIT Press, 29).

xvi   "… hands, tools, and brains, became reciprocally modified by positive feedback loops, as if trying to keep up with each other. A newly invented tool, say a spear, would need a particular design of hand and arm to be used in the most effective way, so that design would be henceforth selected for."

xvii   "psadatephelomy" arises from James Joyce's *Finnegan's Wake* & alludes to divisions, e.g., "the past and present … and present and absent and past and present and perfect. … "

xvii   This module is peopled by Walter Benjamin.

xix   The following 'enterprise' components all qualify as Hinge Operatives: initiate, install, installation, enter, entrance, trance, clearance, elsewhere, open & circumference.

xx   Ananda K. Coomaraswamy, *The Symbolism of Archery*

xxi   For further information on 'Trance Formation' see "Delve/Immerse-Into," *Wrack Lariat* (Black Widow Press) p.205. Also *The Jivin' Ladybug* interview #1.

xxii   See *Wrack Lariat* (BWP), 325. Also, *tenebraed* (BWP), 69.

xxiii   See *Wrack Lariat*, 220.

xxiv   See *tenebraed*, 102.

xxv   Go to Bonnie Lynch Vessels, bonnie-lynch-r9pr.squarespace.com/

xxvi   The Mongols did not have an infantry. They fought from horseback. The bow was their weapon of choice.

xxvii   This is an opportunity to illustrate how 'splintering' (see Spray, 7) bundles into constellations of highly volatile Refractive Impregnations: we now witness *roam, slippage, trespass, stray, meander, saunter, stroll, drift, girdle* (to mention a few) gather momentum & complexity as they compound in Intimate Interosculation. There is such a 'closeness' among these word-clusters, a 'brushing shoulders' tactility, that I would be inclined, except for the associations, to term their relationship familial. Perhaps tribal?

xxviii See above.

xxix Playing/exploring the terms "geodetic precession" and "frame [which I've converted to "flame"] dragging" which are two relativistic events that Gravity Probe B measured to verify some of Einstein's predictions. see Govert Schilling's, *Ripples In Spacetime,* The Belknap Press, Cambridge, Mass., 2017, p.55. Also note, on p.55, how the term "drift" is employed & compare.

xxx Jack Weatherford (*Ghengis Khan and the Making of the Modern World*) writes: "Through the centuries on the rolling, grassy steppes of inner Asia, a warrior-herder carried a Spirit Banner, called a *sulde,* constructed by tying strands of hair from his best stallions to the shaft of a spear just below its blade. Whenever he erected his camp, the warrior planted the Spirit Banner outside the entrance to proclaim his identity and to stand as his perpetual guardian. The Spirit Banner always remained in the open air beneath the Eternal Blue Sky that the Mongols worshipped. As the strands of hair blew and tossed in the nearly constant breeze of the steppe, they captured the power of the wind, the sky, and the sun, and the banner channeled this power from nature to the warrior. The wind in the horsehair inspired the warrior's dreams and encouraged him to pursue his own destiny. ... The union between the man and his Spirit Banner grew so intertwined that when he died, the warrior's spirit was said to reside forever in those tufts of horsehair. While the warrior lived, the horsehair banner carried his destiny; in death, it became his soul."

xxxi Burkhun Khaldun was considered a Sacred Mountain in the Kentii Mountain range of Northeastern Mongolia.

TITLES FROM BLACK WIDOW PRESS
TRANSLATION SERIES

A Life of Poems, Poems of a Life
by Anna de Noailles. Translated by Norman R.
Shapiro. Introduction by Catherine Perry.

Approximate Man and Other Writings by Tristan
Tzara. Translated and edited by Mary Ann Caws.

Art Poétique by Guillevic.
Translated by Maureen Smith.

The Big Game by Benjamin Péret.
Translated with an introduction by Marilyn Kallet.

Boris Vian Invents Boris Vian: A Boris Vian Reader.
Edited and translated by Julia Older.

Capital of Pain by Paul Eluard. Translated by Mary
Ann Caws, Patricia Terry, and Nancy Kline.

Chanson Dada: Selected Poems by Tristan Tzara.
Translated with an introduction and essay
by Lee Harwood.

Earthlight (Clair de Terre) by André Breton.
Translated by Bill Zavatsky and Zack Rogow.
(New and revised edition.)

*Essential Poems and Writings of Joyce Mansour:
A Bilingual Anthology.* Translated with an
introduction by Serge Gavronsky.

Essential Poems and Prose of Jules Laforgue.
Translated and edited by Patricia Terry.

*Essential Poems and Writings of Robert Desnos:
A Bilingual Anthology.* Edited with an introduction
and essay by Mary Ann Caws.

EyeSeas (Les Ziaux) by Raymond Queneau.
Translated with an introduction by Daniela Hurezanu
and Stephen Kessler.

Fables in a Modern Key by Pierre Coran.
Translated by Norman R. Shapiro. Full-color
illustrations by Olga Pastuchiv.

Fables of Town & Country by Pierre Coran.
Translated by Norman R. Shapiro. Full-color
illustrations by Olga Pastuchiv.

Forbidden Pleasures: New Selected Poems 1924–1949
by Luis Cernuda. Translated by Stephen Kessler.

Furor and Mystery & Other Writings by René Char.
Translated by Mary Ann Caws and Nancy Kline.

*The Gentle Genius of Cécile Périn: Selected Poems
(1906–1956).* Edited and translated by
Norman R. Shapiro.

Guarding the Air: Selected Poems of Gunnar Harding.
Translated and edited by Roger Greenwald.

I Have Invented Nothing: Selected Poems
by Jean-Pierre Rosnay. Translated by J. Kates.

The Inventor of Love & Other Writings
by Gherasim Luca. Translated by Julian & Laura
Semilian. Introduction by Andrei Codrescu.
Essay by Petre Răileanu.

Jules Supervielle: Selected Prose and Poetry.
Translated by Nancy Kline & Patricia Terry.

La Fontaine's Bawdy by Jean de La Fontaine.
Translated with an introduction by
Norman R. Shapiro.

Last Love Poems of Paul Eluard.
Translated with an introduction by Marilyn Kallet.

Love, Poetry (L'amour la poésie) by Paul Eluard.
Translated with an essay by Stuart Kendall.

Pierre Reverdy: Poems, Early to Late.
Translated by Mary Ann Caws and Patricia Terry.

Poems of André Breton: A Bilingual Anthology.
Translated with essays by Jean-Pierre Cauvin
and Mary Ann Caws.

Poems of A.O. Barnabooth by Valery Larbaud.
Translated by Ron Padgett and Bill Zavatsky.

Poems of Consummation by Vicente Aleixandre.
Translated by Stephen Kessler.

Préversities: A Jacques Prévert Sampler.
Translated and edited by Norman R. Shapiro.

The Sea and Other Poems by Guillevic.
Translated by Patricia Terry. Introduction by
Monique Chefdor.

To Speak, to Tell You? Poems by Sabine Sicaud.
Translated by Norman R. Shapiro. Introduction
and notes by Odile Ayral-Clause.

MODERN POETRY SERIES

ABC of Translation by Willis Barnstone

An Alchemist with One Eye on Fire
by Clayton Eshleman

An American Unconscious by Mebane Robertson

Anticline by Clayton Eshleman

Archaic Design by Clayton Eshleman

Backscatter: New and Selected Poems by John Olson

Barzakh (Poems 2000–2012) by Pierre Joris

The Caveat Onus by Dave Brinks

City Without People: The Katrina Poems
by Niyi Osundare

Clayton Eshleman/The Essential Poetry: 1960–2015

Concealments and Caprichos by Jerome Rothenberg

Crusader-Woman by Ruxandra Cesereanu.
Translated by Adam J. Sorkin. Introduction by Andrei
Codrescu.

Curdled Skulls: Poems of Bernard Bador.
Translated by Bernard Bador with
Clayton Eshleman.

Dada Budapest by John Olson

Disenchanted City (La ville désenchantée)
by Chantal Bizzini. Translated by J. Bradford
Anderson, Darren Jackson, and Marilyn Kallet.

Endure: Poems by Bei Dao.
Translated by Clayton Eshleman and Lucas Klein.

Exile Is My Trade: A Habib Tengour Reader.
Translated by Pierre Joris.

Eye of Witness: A Jerome Rothenberg Reader.
Edited with commentaries by Heriberto Yepez
& Jerome Rothenberg.

Fire Exit by Robert Kelly

Forgiven Submarine
by Ruxandra Cesereanu and Andrei Codrescu

Fractal Song by Jerry W. Ward, Jr.

from stone this running by Heller Levinson

Grindstone of Rapport: A Clayton Eshleman Reader

The Hexagon by Robert Kelly

How Our Bodies Learned by Marilyn Kallet

Larynx Galaxy by John Olson

LinguaQuake by Heller Levinson

The Love That Moves Me by Marilyn Kallet

Memory Wing by Bill Lavender

Packing Light: New and Selected Poems
by Marilyn Kallet

Penetralia by Clayton Eshleman

The Present Tense of the World: Poems 2000–2009
by Amina Saïd. Translated with an introduction by
Marilyn Hacker.

The Price of Experience by Clayton Eshleman

The Secret Brain: Selected Poems 1995–2012
by Dave Brinks

Signal from Draco: New and Selected Poems
by Mebane Robertson

Soraya (Sonnets) by Anis Shivani

Tenebraed by Heller Levinson

Wrack Lariat by Heller Levinson

Forthcoming title:
Garage Elegies by Stephen Kessler

LITERARY THEORY /
BIOGRAPHY SERIES

*Barbaric Vast & Wild: A Gathering of Outside and
Subterranean Poetry (Poems for the Millennium,
vol. 5).* Editors: Jerome Rothenberg and
John Bloomberg-Rissman

Clayton Eshleman: The Whole Art by Stuart Kendall

Revolution of the Mind: The Life of André Breton
by Mark Polizzotti

WWW.BLACKWIDOWPRESS.COM